While Morning Stars Sang

An Anthology of Poetry and Verse

TABBY HOUSE BOOKS
Volume One
Edited by Linda G. Salisbury

Dorothy Blanchard Bennett
Alison Denight
Lucille Hicks

Juanita Beresford-Redman
Mary Paxton "Pax" Kirby
Nancy B. Miller

For Chris,
Enjoy!

Nancy

Manufactured in the United States of America
Library of Congress Number: 91-066376
ISBN: 0-9627974-4-8

TABBY HOUSE BOOKS

4429 Shady Lane, Charlotte Harbor, FL 33980
813-629-7646 • 813-627-6938

Contents

"Time is but the stream I go a-fishing in. I drink at it; but while I drink I see the sandy bottom and detect how shallow it is. Its thin current slides away, but eternity remains. I would drink deeper; fish in the sky whose bottom is pebbly with stars."

— Thoreau

". . . while the morning stars sang together and all the angels shouted for joy . . ."

— Job 38:7

Nancy B. Miller

Nancy B. Miller grew up on Long Island, New York and first wrote poetry for her fourth grade play.

At Manhasset High School she was enamored of Robert Frost, Emily Dickinson and e.e. cummings. At Oberlin College her poetic tastes turned to W.H. Auden, William Carlos Williams, Denise Levertov and Shakespearean sonnets.

Later, she co-edited "The OWL and the Peacock," Ohio Wesleyan University's literary magazine. Nancy graduated cum laude in 1967 with a B.A. in English, receiving the F.L. Hunt Poetry Award.

A former teacher of Latin and English, she now teaches Suzuki Violin, is a member of the Reading Symphony and works in the Music Department of Phillips Academy, Andover. Nancy and her husband, Donald, live in North Reading, Massachusetts with children: Sandy, Cynthia and Tom.

When the Muse is in Residence...

Poems wait in line
>> Like shoppers
>> In long, weary Saturday supermarket lines
>> Children howling for watermelon Bubble Yum
>> Mom searching for fifty cent cereal coupon
>> Universal Bar decoder bleeps:
>>> One item at a time
>>> One item at a time
>>> One item at a time

Poems wait in line
>> Like skiers
>> Ropes and stanchions cordon off this mittened
>>> Gortex-ed, Rossignol-ed group
>> They wait, scarfs moistened from the breathing
>>> into them.
>> Some, brazen, anticipating steep, black diamond trails;
>> Others hoping for the peace of easier
>>> green circle choices.
>> The triple chair, hungry for three bundled
>>> bodies, hairpin turns inside its dark house.

Poems wait in line
>> Like travelers
>> Suitcases filled with expectations, intentions,
>> Clothing to cover, to decorate, to enliven.
>> Some patient, knowing their seat is assigned;
>> Some anxious, not sure of their place.

Letting Go..

Two neighbors owned two dogs, same litter born,
Retrievers, honey golden, bound to love.
One owner bound and tied his pet above
His yard; He penned and fenced the dog forlorn.
The other, not as fearful of a loss,
Allowed his friend to run unleashed and then
Return when whistled for. Now would a pen
Prevent a loss of that first dog? Across
The yard I saw him jump the fence and flee.
I dreamt my beat up patchwork quilt I gave
To raffle at a soccer dance. The bidding
Done, my friend bestowed it back to me

    Hold tight to things they soon escape or flee;
    To own, let go, they will come back to thee.

Ruth's Monologue at my Grandmother's Funeral

"Now don't you all worry about Florence
being lonely under all them flowers...
That's the last thing...
Well, she wanted to come Home don't ya know,
      all these winter days.
             And she wrote me that.
You all look so nice;
She'd be proud of you, you know. You look nice.
      Some might say I dressed too loud for the
      occasion.
      But you know how she was.
      She always liked this red hat.
      It wasn't often I dressed up—
      And when I did, she liked that.

"Imagine you folks won't be getting up this way much
anymore...
Sort of out of your way, I know.
But Florence'll be all right.
      I told her last November, I said,
      'Florence, you go East for the Winter and
      Be with your people.
      That's only right.
      Then, come spring you'll be back
      working in your rose garden
      and scrubbing your front porch steps.'
        (She always wanted things 'just so' you know.)

"Then she'd get discouraged
on account of her illness and that.
And I'd say,
            'Florence, you'll live longer than me.
            Why you'll live longer than Harriet, I bet'
            (And Harriet is 97 now. Still in that 'home'
            down to Painesville, and gone mental.
            But our funeral home has her buryin' clothes—
            they say they're splendid—
            all hanging in a room upstairs.

"She'd be down-hearted those November days.
And I'd say,
            'Florence, you'll be back in April;
            and we'll take a drive out to see Clarence
            (Clarence was out to the funeral home last
            night;
            did you see him?),
            and down the gorge to see the white dogwood
            and over to town to buy some yard goods.
"Those was all campaign promises, a course
(like the promises Pa made to Ma about the carriage
horse, so Ma'd agree to marry him and that)
But it seemed to give her strength.

"Well, now it's May a course,
not April.
But Florence has come Home,
And don't you folks worry—
she won't be in for any loneliness this Spring.
Why, my John's just three plots over.
And only in the ground a year
(God rest his soul).
I visit him most every day and tell him
what goes on.

      Florence would have thought it's sentimental
      but my John likes to hear
      what goes on.
      Always did.
      (Only time I 'member him deliberately turning
      off that hearing aid was two years ago
      Christmas when the grandchildren were here.)

 "Now don't go worrying 'cause
I'll talk to Florence everytime I come
to see my John.
And she has her Clyde. He's right there next.
She's missed him these seventeen years.
Now don't you go worrying.
Florence was proud of the lot of you.
She wouldn't have you fret."

And We Will All Be Changed

At nine fifty-two,
I went to pick some parsley for the meatloaf.
At the top of the porch stairs I felt
A presence.
A butterfly on the fat yellow marigold was slowly,
          silently, pulsing his wings—
          dreamily
A fall butterfly—orange and brown like the
chrysanthemums
in the driftwood boxes.
Not especially spectacular.
A touch small.
And fragile.
For eternity that butterfly pulsated slowly.
          The wind whispered in the trees out of respect.
          A crow jeered.
          Locusts sang.
And then away it flew.
(Did my coming prompt its leaving?)
Up over the porch rail
Resting briefly on the down spout
Over the roof and gone.

First Loss

Fish floating, belly up in the small glass fish bowl.
A boy's own first pet.

Shiny and sleek like a wet, orange goldie on the beach,
      just kissed by a wave,
This little fish looks perfect enough.
No bruises or gashes, no pallor.
Perfect fish whose eyes are still open,
      Why do you float on the top of this fish bowl?

The nine year old boy tries to lift the still
goldness out of the tepid water.
But through his damp eyes and warm face,
      he cannot make the stainless soup ladle hold
      the slipperiness.

He buries his face in my yellow apron.
      The soup ladle drips on the clean tile.
How golden and slippery life is.
Sometimes we don't even try to scoop it up
      until it is floating motionless.

Passage

Young Adam at camp.
Good-bye to a Hera mom.
A new world awaits him
Mountains
A pupa-stage mosquito netting tucked neatly
      into the Ninja Turtle sleeping sack
A path to the lake
      troubled by snaking roots
      small slithering, snakes
      tree discarded birchbark.
A mirror lake, formerly volcanic;
      never have its depths been fathomed;
      even sonar fails.
Adam has left his grassy yard,
      his frisbee chasing golden retriever
      his climbing tree
      for
Mountains
And he does not want to be there.
A passage.
He wants to come home now.
What shall we tell him?
Tell him to find what he likes to do,
And do a lot of that.

Healing

As I peeled potatoes
Even, thumb-shaped, brown skins slipped from
       white naked, cold-water roundness.
Then slipped the knife,
my second finger sliced.
Red mixed with ordinary beige,
Extraordinary crimson dripping into my porcelain sink.
Cold water,
Ice cold numbness on the wound,
Diluted blood.
But from that moment—healing!
In a day the crevice closed.
Drew into itself for strength.
I watched daily as this finger mended.
It needed no instruction,
This Divine plan of healing,
Reconstruction for a single finger tip.

Crimson heart that has pumped pain throughout my body,
Learn from this finger tip.

A Talisman

Ivan was faced with monsters in that wood
A swirling dance of savage, driving beat;
Syncopated, xylophonic feet
To trample on his heart; But nearby stood
The Firebird with feather to protect
The boy from psychic danger. Could it be
That Dorothy on her way to Oz would see
That shoes of red could gain her self respect
Sufficient to protect from Western Witch
who tried to dash her faith? In journeys past
Dark monsters, wicked witch or cliff, hold fast
to feather or red shoes: one's power can switch.

    The feather, special shoes a luck imparts;
    A talisman does lighten darkened hearts.

Do I Remember Being One Week Old

Twelve, Moby Dick-sized, almond-colored fish,
Reassuring presence,
Swim toward me.
Deep in the murky ocean
Twelve in semi-circle,
Semi-circle around me,
Alien that I am in these deep waters.
Curious, all of us stare.
But the twelve have no eyes.
Yet they see through me
    with their eyeless almond being.

Snowflakes Rule

Standing in front of the garage,
We look up at the snowflakes —
For a moment
Human Beings
Not Human Doings.
Each flake swirls, pirouettes, spirals down and down.
Catch one.
White against the grey.
Shadow of a plane above.
Large bird humming speed, direction, goals, progress.
For this moment, goals are the shadow.
Snowflakes rule.

Luke 12:25

A girl lies broken on the overpass
Clothed in velvet collared wool coat
      with matching fur-trimmed hat,
She lies motionless, eyes wide,
      next to my muddied car.
I rush to save her severed arm —
      to keep it clean.
      Is there a clean towel for wrapping?
Motorists whizz by.
The driver of my Voyager wipes the dirt from the headlight.
Now I pick up the arm.
      The broken end is the end of a pipe.
      The pipe is covered over, sealed.

The child does not cry.
There is no blood.
Motorists whizz by.

Perhaps this arm is vital
Perhaps it is not.

I shall keep it clean, just in case.

Mary Paxton "Pax" Kirby

Pax Kirby contributes poetry and verse from her unpublished book, *Jingles for the Jangled*. Her work reflects her witty and insightful look at life from the perspective of successful writer, radio and television director at a Park Avenue advertising agency, and singer. She is also a mother who loves her sons and grandchildren, and is the beloved wife of radio and television star Durward Kirby. Her talents also include painting, mostly portraits.

In 1983 she published her successful and charming book, *The View from Under the Table,* an authoritative look at the Kirby household by their poodle, Bonnie. Mel Crawford, internationally known illustrator, provided the art for that book and for selected poems in this volume.

The Kirbys spend their winters in Florida and their summers in Connecticut.

Love Before First Sight

(for Spencer Cooper Kirby before his birth)

I have never seen him.
I don't know if his eyes
Are green or blue.
I only know...I love him.

He will come to me from
some far off cosmic place,
Away beyond my ken,
Known only to God, not men.

There are certain things
I am sure about him
that make me know it will be love...
Even before first sight

It is written
That we shall love.
It is in his stars.
It is my destiny.

He will arrive in the light
Of the bright August moon
I await his coming
With arms open wide.

Oh, how long I have waited
For this son of my son.
God, please heap blessings
On my precious grandson.

God Bless This Child

(written for Alexander Daniel Kirby before his birth)

A new little life is on its way
May it greet the world on a sunny day.
May the skies be blue as the baby's eyes,
On the day it sees its first sunrise.

God grant that this baby be perfect and strong.
Give this child a happy life and one that's long.
Bless it with a lively mind.
Make it gentle, loving, kind.

Let it live in a world of peace on earth
From the very first day of this child's birth.
May it inherit all good from its Mother and Dad.
May it face life bravely and seldom be sad.

God, please bless it with beautiful features
And abiding love for all Your creatures.
Let this child bring its parents bountiful joy,
Be it a little girl or a baby boy.
God bless this child.

24

I Looked to the Hills

Early one morning when I arose from my bed,
I sat by my window. As my Bible had said,
I looked over the still lake and up to the hills.
I was hoping to find ease from all of my ills.
I prayed that up there my God I would find,
To heal my spirit, my body, my mind.

When He wasn't there, I closed my eyes.
Gone were the hills...all my earthly ties.
To the land, the birds, the flowers, the trees;
All of the world that one usually sees.
In that velvety darkness, I looked deep inside
And found Him...where the quiet and soul abide.

Who Said, Nothing Rhymes With Orange?

As I behold the purple finch
I know one thing that is a cinch,
As he flutters up within our range
He's mostly brown and sometimes orange
Believe me, let it here be said
He is not purple he is red.
Whoever named him, in my mind,
Surely must have been colorblind.

Lost Children

A stranger...with sadness in her eyes,
Revealed to me,
Unexpectedly,
The reason for her inward cries.
Her little son was dead at five.
No longer alive...and only five.

I thought of my children whom I love so dear.
Not babies, but grown,
Now men... my own.
Then suddenly knowledge came
Loud and clear.
My babies have been gone for
Many a year.

We exchange each little child
For someone who's grown up.
Some stray away, as far as the moon.
Like that sad little mother,
We all soon have to give up
Our tiny children...
Too soon...much too soon.

Spring is a Yearning

Spring is a yearning.

Felt keenest in February,
When sleet and snow
Pile up endlessly...
And you want them to GO!

Spring is a yearning.

It's a yen for warmth and air,
Soft scented air.
Not heat, contrived by man;
Fresh air, moved
Gently on by nature's fan.

Spring is a yearning.

It's restless, an ache,
Felt deep down in your heart.
For winter to leave
And one green bud to start.

Spring is a yearning.

It's the desire to conjure
Up a flower or to hear a bird's song.
It gives pain to think...
How long they've been gone.

The Chickadee

This has been my observation,
Watching at a feeding station.
The chickadee, a tiny mite,
Is swift and darting in his flight.
He comes to the feeder and waits his turn,
From greedy birds who never learn,
To make a little bit of space,
For someone else to take a place.
They fight and push and crowd and shove,
Without a shred of selfless love.

The Chickadee sits and waits so sweetly,
For them to gorge themselves completely,
Somewhere inside it is innate,
For him to bide his time and wait.
When it is his turn to fill his need,
The little darling takes just one seed.
He flies away with it to a tree.
A lesson perhaps for you and me?
A Chickadee knows it's only right,
For everybody to be polite.

She Loves Me

Her love for me is beyond conception.
Unparalleled without exception.
She gives me all of her attention.
Her lapses are too slight to mention.
She's single-minded in her devotion.
Her eyes shine bright with deep emotion.
She loves me when I'm wide awake,
And when I sleep she's there to take
Care of me from every harm.
In bed, she snuggles, keeps me warm.
She loves me truly, like no other,
Sister, brother, kids or mother.
Oh, it's so very plain to see,
She gives her love to only me.
Other people may come around,
But when they do she turns them down.
She gaily greets them but lets me know
She's mine again when at last they go.
Who is capable of so much love?
Was sent to me from heav'n above?
Who means the world and all to me?
My tiny poodle. Her name? Mimi!

Hooray for Faye

There was a sensitive young lady
Whose name was Faye.
Lost her job as a checker
In a market one day.

She made perfect change,
Didn't waste anyone's time.
She was fired from her job
For committing one crime.

She simply refused
Insincerely to say
To the people who passed her...
"Have a good day!"

At the Super-Market

Grocery shopping can become an ordeal,
Especially when your cart has one flat wheel.
Pushing through crowded aisles can be rough.
With four wheels working it's tough enough.

I can cope with this but what I really hate,
Is standing in long lines when I'm running late.
When I'm in a hurry, I'm a nervous wreck,
Waiting at the check-out counter bottleneck.

Inching along, with my cart piled high,
I have an appointment, I heave a sigh.
As I approach the front of my row,
It always happens, wouldn't you know!

The manager's called in a loud nasal tone.
It's a sound that all checkers seem to be prone.
She tells him he's wanted at counter nine.
Whatever the number...it's bound to be mine.

The man is never where he should be.
There's no sign of him that I can see.
The woman ahead of me has bought out the store.
She fumbles in her handbag and holds us up more.

I knew it!
I knew it!
It invariably gives me a pain in the neck.
Again! I'm behind someone writing a check.

"A Wife's Retirement"

You fell in love and married HIM.
You knew your love would never dim.
You did the very best you could.
All the things a good wife should.

You raised your kids, you joined a pool
So every one could get to school.
You saw that they were clean and well fed.
You heard their prayers when they went to bed.

You chauffeured them to dancing schools,
To dentists and to swimming pools.
You had hot dinners on the table
When HE got home, if He was able.

You took the kids to wishing wells
And rode with them on a carrousels.
When it was time for recreation
You all went off on a vacation.

HE rented you a summer cottage
Where it was you in charge of pottage.
You cleaned the house and made the beds,
Untangled little curly heads.

You did the work without complaining
Even on days when it was raining.
You <u>knew</u> you'd change this whole Environment.
The day would come with HIS retirement.

That wonderful day has finally arrived.
You've worked all your life but you both survived.
Now HE's on the golf course or HE's out fishin'.
What happened to YOU?...You're still in the kitchen!

Dorothy Parker, Out-dated

"Men seldom make passes
At girls who wear glasses,"
said Dorothy Parker in her bright, flippant way.
She couldn't get away with that old quote today.

The girls of the 90's have learned how to zap,
That out-dated, over-rated handicap.
They don't worry about what covers their eyes.
They care more about what un-covers their thighs.

They wear tiny strings, that bare their bottoms and tops;
As little as they can without bringing the cops.
They know that the fellows no longer check...
Anything that goes on...above the neck!

The Movie Kiss

Nowadays, you know what I miss?
The good old fashioned movie kiss.
When Clark Gable took a girl in his arms.
And kissed her gently on the lips.
In the darkened theater on the movie screen,
It made my youthful heart turn flips.

When did this kiss go out of fashion,
Turn into such an over-blown passion?
Something I can just hardly abide
Is when they kiss with their mouths open wide.
When they perform this unsanitary antic,
It takes away everything that is romantic.

The love story that has held me rapt,
By this device, has just been zapped!
Although it's meant to be exotic,
Senses stirring and erotic,
It only gives me an attack of the squirms.
All I can think of is mouthwash and germs!

On the Town in Beverly Hills

We went to dinner in Beverly Hills.
The memory of it lingers still.
All dressed up for the festivities,
Hoping to see some real celebrities.

Our place was reserved at the famous Bistro,
Where so many of the well known often go.
A lot of them seem to have proclivities,
To see and be seen by other celebrities.

One in awhile they get some kind of a charge,
Being recognized by the public at large.
Directors, producers and today's so called "stars,"
Rolled up to the door in expensive foreign cars.

Ushered to tables, as each took his place,
I didn't recognize a single face.
Then all of a sudden the Bistro lit up.
A lady and gentleman came into sup.

They came in with quiet dignity,
As unobtrusive as they could be.
Unassuming and handsome, he seated his wife
And gave me the biggest thrill of my life.

I sat up with a start and craned my neck.
The first time I laid eyes on Gregory Peck.

What's Going On Outside?

With deep apologies to Willard Scott.
A personality we like a lot.
There's a problem that has always been,
Peculiar to T.V. weathermen.
They are up on isotopes and cloud formations,
Wind directions noted, for navigation.

But when they give us late weather news,
They sometimes only serve to confuse.
They say the day will be bright and sunny.
I take a look and say, "Gee, that's funny!"
My nice clean window panes are staining.
Where I'm sitting—boy! It's raining!

They could correct this mistake so easily.
It seems to be so very simple to me.
If just before they gave final predictions
Using only scientific convictions,
They would step to the window, open it wide,
And take a good look at the weather outside!

The Soda Fountain

Sometimes when I walk into a drugstore,
I think of the fixtures that are no more.
I used to find them impossible to resist.
It's the soda fountains that no longer exist.

I recall the days I came in to get cool,
And climbed up on top of a spinning stool.
I leaned upon a marble counter,
Where a friend or two I might encounter.

Nothing can compare to that old time pleasure,
Of passing a few moments of idle leisure,
Having an ice cold Coca Cola,
Or a delicious chocolate soda.

They were concocted right before your very eyes,
While you were sitting there so you could supervise.
Your mouth would water, your taste buds would stir up,
While you said, "Please, go heavy on the syrup!"

Nothing in a can or bottle tastes so nice,
As an old fashioned Coke with lots of chipped ice.
The old soda fountains got the sack.
Oh, how I wish they would bring them back.

Thoughts in a Jacuzzi

Some times when I have nothing to do,
My empty mind lets thoughts wander through.
The other morning, while in the jacuzzi,
One ran by me that was really a doozie.
It got in my way,
For most of the day.
It's almost too ridiculous to put into words,
To tell you I was wondering, who first named the birds.

Did Eve ask Adam, "Dear, what is that flying?"
Did he give it a name? Or without trying
To put a name to the thing, above his head,
Did he just shrug his shoulders and go to bed?
How many centuries were to go by,
Before anyone thought to give it a try?
See what happens when you let your brain get lazy?
Vagrant thoughts like this can just drive you crazy.

A Fear of Lightning

I have a dog who doesn't like lightning.
To her, it's a thing that is dreadfully frightening.
At the very first rumble of distant thunder,
She looks for a place that she can get under.

She seems to know far in advance,
When the skies are about to dance
With jagged, angry streaks of light.
She senses that it's time for flight.

She's not afraid of man or beast.
Nothing scares her in the least.
But when she hears the thunder boom,
She holes up in a darkened room.

She surely is afraid to hang,
Around when things are going BANG!
She totally hates the Fourth of July,
When all the loud fireworks shoot up the sky.

I follow her wherever she goes,
To comfort her, because, goodness knows,
It's easy for me to give her sympathy;
Deep in my heart I have so much empathy.

When those dark clouds begin to form,
I'm scared, too—of a thunderstorm.
She is the only legitimate excuse I can think of,
For a grown woman to duck something that <u>she</u> is afraid of!

Running Off at the Mouth

There is a man I met, last winter, down south,
Who has a case of running off at the mouth.
In any small group or at a big celebration,
He manages to take over all conversation.

He always figures some smart way to devise,
To keep you from getting a word in edgewise.
He has endless stories that he will tell you.
He drones on and on, and begins to bore you.

You can't get away from him, your time he'll consume.
He will follow you if you walk out of the room.
If, at last, you duck him in some dark hall...
He will keep right on talking...to the wall.

He doesn't know the meaning of repartee.
Thinks others have nothing that's worthy to say.
One night, to his wife, he guiltily inquired,
"My dear, do you think I talked more than required?"

His silent partner looked up in surprise...
And gave him an answer that was so wise.
"Let's put it this way," she said as she turned.
"Tell me, tonight dear, what have you learned?"

Lucille Hicks

 Author and poet Lucille Hicks' motto is "It's never too late," and her life exemplifies those words. In retirement she became a college student. At age 70, Lucille was in the first graduating class of West Virginia Wesleyan's Charlotte County branch in 1983, receiving her Bachelor of Liberal Studies degree.

A native of Battle Creek, Michigan, she moved to Southwest Florida 22 years ago. She has three children, 10 grandchildren and 15 great grandchildren. She sets the educational pace for them as she continues to audit courses at Florida Southern College in Lake Suzy.

Aside from her prolific writing, Lucille is active in her church; the American Association of University Women (from which she received the 1991 Educational Foundation award), and other community clubs and organizations.

She has written a book, *Stamp A White Horse*, and is a contributor to poetry books and magazines. Her pen and ink drawings illustrate her Haiku poems.

Haiku—my flights of fancy

   Haiku is a Japanese poem consisting of three unrhymed
lines which contain respectively five-seven-five syllables. According
to my reading, the ideal Haiku presents two varied images,
one indicating a general condition, the other a momentary
perception. Originally the subject dealt with man con-
fronting nature. Modern North American Haiku often
deals with human nature in a humorous or satirical
manner. It takes two to make a Haiku, the writer and
the reader. The writer shows an experience and
leaves the conclusion to the readers' imagination.
Not all of the following poems agree with the rules of
true Haiku. They are my flights of fancy.

— Lucille Hicks

The sea gull swoops low
drops a mussel from his beak
dines from broken shell

A wedge of wild geese
vibrant against the morning sky
marks nature's time clock

Bracing with his tail
he hammers on tree trunks
woodpeckers—hole in one

In the wet earth
at the edge of the water
incised deer tracks

Tracks of summer sun
catch dust motes in slow action
a kaleidoscope

Diamonds caught in space
held apart with strips of lead
Tiffany in glass

Flock of clucking hens
makes chicken coop quite noisy
women's club meeting

Crowded chicken coop
needs more space for flock
Kentucky Fried Chicken

Stew bubbling in iron pot
potatoes baked in the ashes
microwaveless past

Sudden thunder clap
as piercing as the still air
leaves drop soundlessly

After the storm
air feels as if
dipped in crushed ice

Snow chasing the air
catching nothing but
ears and collars

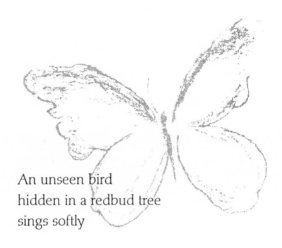

An unseen bird
hidden in a redbud tree
sings softly

The sky a blue mat
for white clouds
wind inflated

Stalks of silver sage
gray leaves of dusty miller
the roadside parade

Hear my loneliness
termites chewing on a board
The hole grows larger

The attic is full
treasure and trash mixed together
serendipity

In the warm kitchen
lamplight for comfort
we draw together

Flies flies obnoxious flies
only one safe place for you
sit on a fly swatter

Pie cake sugary treats
are all on the no-no list
now — to eat my words

Hawaiian dancers
sway slither and shake
Jello in a dish

Sun catches the tree tops
casting shadows on the lawn
lacy mantilla

Over stone it flows
making music as it goes
rippling rhythm river

October's brisk winds
downs leaves from maple trees
colorful strip tease

Be wary little crab
bury yourself in deep sand
legs are good eating

Driftwood
bleached white as bone
skeleton of former self

The kelp
dark green and black
smells of salt

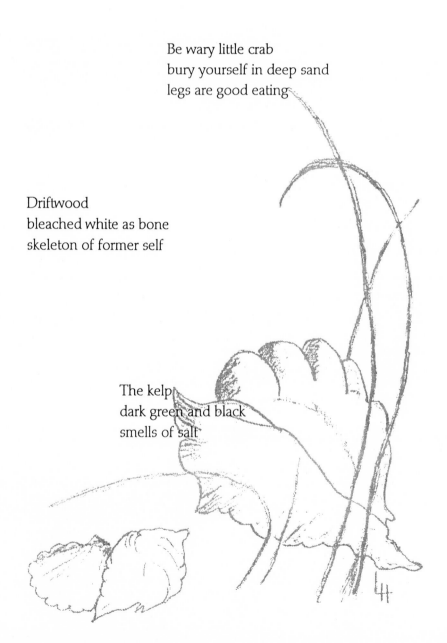

Juanita Beresford-Redman

 Juanita Beresford-Redman's life can be said to be an open book. She describes herself as addicted to words and writing and has surrounded herself with the printed word all her life.

A native of New York City, Juanita received her B.A. from Marymount College, and her M.S. from Columbia University. An avid reader, her logical career choice was to become a librarian—first in acquistions at Manhattanville College in Purchase, New York, then as a school librarian in Suffern, New York.

During the 20 years that she and her husband, David, lived in northern New Jersey, Juanita was active in the community and school affairs and co-founded the Woodcliff Lake Book Group. Currently a resident of Englewood, Florida, she sings, writes book reviews and is assistant director of the Englewood Area Writer's Guild.

Juanita and David have one son, Bruce, and one dog, Cinnamon.

Deception

Softly falls the rain
Upon the hardened earth.
As if to regain
The long-forgotten spring
It eagerly receives
This nourishment which brings
A fast-succeeding dearth
Of life. Soft rain deceives.

* * *

First, winter comes.

Dream Traveller

I walk a shabby, cobbled street
In a village aged and still.
Emptiness echoes in the chill
Of shuttered shops, deserted homes.
My bones are hollow cores of cold
More brittle with each step.
No wind; no sound relieves the agony.
A glow appears — a store apulse
With stroboscopic light. The brightness
Fades to neon as I near.
Behind its pane stand candle saints
With halos made of wick. I strike
A match and through the glass ignite
Each righteous head. My hand slides out—
A thousand stinging sparks descend.
The icons drip, grimace, reform,
Then burn with inquisition's flame.
I warm my magus' hand against the blaze.

Gemini

Our lives, begun as one
And now so disparate grown,
Betray a weakness in the chain.
Once uniquely similar —
Now similar in that we are unique.

There is constraint, unease,
That restlessness one feels
With someone that he loves
Yet cannot understand,
Or loves while understanding
And is guilty
For the limits of such love.

You are my shadow there,
Uncertain and unloved,
Seeking reverence
For what we were —
Not seeing what you have become.

Imagine That—A Cat

I'd like to be a Siamese cat.
—At least that's what I think—
'Though I wouldn't wish my eyes to cross
Or my tail to have a kink.

My world would glow in sapphire blue
—Albeit at a slant—
My toilette would be elegant,
My bearing arrogant.

One born to feline royalty
Must play her proper role;
I'd dine on shrimp and lobster tails
From a jewel-encrusted bowl.

My ancestors were idolized
As goddesses, I hear;
They lounged about the temple steps
Content with their career.

And on their necks, the temple mark,
—I'd surely have one, too—
Where they were picked up by a god
In B.C. CCCII.

Oh, there would be a chosen few
On whom I'd deign to smile,
I'd serve them spicy tit-bits
And a brew of camomile.

Proprieties would be observed;
My fire-eyes would snap
If any prole should dare suggest
I sit upon his lap.

I'd have a satin cushion-throne
On which they could adore me;
It's just the thing for forty-winks
Should adoration bore me.

Musings

Spring is the season of rebirth,
When sunlight's glow revivifies
The earth and all things grow.
Will it bring my renewal, too?
I wish that I could know
As certainly as nature orders
Season's cyclic flow.

The Silversmith

Dedicated to the memory of "Bill" Ives

> Flashes of light—
> Brilliant, blinding—
> Refract, reflect as it moves.
> Mirage;
> A shimmering image whose
> Hand-hammered curves sweep up,
> Turn, gleam, take shape,
> Turn again—and dissolve in
> Blue fire!

Synthesize

My mother is dead.
I see my sister everywhere.

A neighbor comes to visit and I see my sister's face.
Questioning eyes, unsure, look back at me,
Innocent yet weary, and so sad.

> ("We'll wait until your sister comes," she said,
> And folded her translucent hands in rest.)

A stranger asks directions and I see my sister's face.
The mouth is young, the lines are deeply drawn,
The chin is soft and aging; it is sad.

> ("It's late now, Mom, and growing dark," I said.
> "Tomorrow, then." She slept her fragile sleep.)

I glimpse a woman's profile and I see my sister's face.
The bones are fine, the skin is loose and pale,
The neck is bent with sorrow. All is sad.

> ("She's here," I said and touched my mother's cheek.
> "At last." She sighed and took my sister's hand.)

I look at my reflection and I see my sister's face.
I see my sister everywhere.
My mother is dead.

Worthington's Cherryripe

The land was theirs by deed
But hers by right.

They knew the house; from root cellar
To cupola—its senescent groans
And creaks, familiar as their own,
Were eased by Franklin's glow.

She knew the pond. She'd sit, alert,
Watch trout sweep-clean their hatchery,
Place every frog where it belonged
And revel in the symmetry.

They knew the town; the lumber mill,
The general store replete with cheddar
Wheel, saw-dusted floor and bench
Where old men watched the world decline.

She knew the field. With boundless joy,
She'd run through yellow trefoil blooms,
And find the perfect spot to watch
The road unravel in the sun.

They knew the church; the origin
Of every stone. Carved on each pew
A name they knew from childhood days.
Rose-window lights remember who have gone.

She knew the woods; the root-cage homes
Of mice and vole—the path through fallen
Birch to higher ground where deer
Made beds of moss and fragrant pine.

Their world was old and hers was ever-new.
The land was hers by right.

Bequest

To live in memory.
Is this our legacy to those we love?
Bereft, we beg
His spirit to remain;
To comfort, to bring pain,
(For in remembering we lose again.)
Is this existence in our thoughts
The only immortality that he
Achieves? Does each of us who grieves,
Who carries in his heart a part
Of him he loved, bestow eternal life?
How fitting if our gift to those who
Gave us life is life beyond all time.

R.S.V.P.

When it was done...
Did you linger?
Did you stay to see his face
Exposed in grief?
Or could you see? Or hear?
Was seeing through a prism—slashed,
Distorted images of glass
Or mist-enveloped shapes in silhouette?
Were there crescendos, strange cacophonies
Or echoes through impenetrable haze?
Could you hear the prayers for you?
The tearing of my brother's heart,
The voice that told his love?

Or was your going swift....

Alison Denight

Poet and short story writer, Alison Denight, one of nine children, grew up in Collingswood, New Jersey. Her love of family and of nature is evident in her varied selections represented here.

A native of North Tonawanda, New York, she has also lived in Massachusetts and Panama, and currently resides in Punta Gorda, Florida where she is active in a number of community organizations and her church. Prior to "retirement," Alison was, for 21 years, an executive secretary with the Public Service Electric & Gas Company of New Jersey. She is now enjoying adult education courses and is an officer of the Peace River Writers' Guild.

Besides writing, she finds time to fish, decorate sand dollars, and collect quotations and Precious Moments figurines.

She is married to Don Denight and has two stepsons.

Awakening

I jumped from my bed
    when the clock struck seven
And went to the window
    to look at God's heaven.

The sun was shining,
    the sky was blue,
I bowed my head and said,
    "God, thank you."

Self-Sought Treasures

Go after and cling to
Only that which is good;
Life's got much to offer
To those who would.

It's more satisfying
And there's much to be had
When you look for the good
Instead of the bad.

Memories of Mom

"Give to the world the best that you have
    and the best will come back to you,"
These were words Mom repeated oft times
    in hopes we would feel that way too.

She lived and laughed and loved a lot
    and referred to her life this way:
"A succession of happy memories
    that were locked in her heart to stay."

Mom reminisced much of the good times shared
    with my Dad, our family and her friends,
And seemed to be ever so grateful
    for each time until its end.

"Unless there are valleys, you don't
    notice the hills,"
Mom talked of, to just let us know,
That God in His wisdom was teaching us all
    in hopes that we might grow.

Her most cherished possession in material form
    that she treasured with all of her heart
Was a picture she kept of our family—
    of each one contributing their part.

Mom wanted to be remembered by all
　　when laid down for her eternal rest
"As an honest, dependable, helpful person—
　　good friend, good sport" — the best!

Her goal in life was to do what she could
　　when others required a hand;
Mom needed to give and wanted to love
　　to achieve what she had planned.

When asked what favorite place she lived
　　Mom answered, "Florida, of course!"
For good reasons too numerous to mention,
　　she being the reliable source.

Mom talked of beautiful things she'd seen
　　and I'd like to mention a few:
Her nine newborn babies, colorful gardens,
　　sunsets and waters of blue

She dearly loved life and admired this world,
　　but said she'd be ready when called
To continue her journey to the Great Beyond;
　　where she's destined to be enrolled.

A woman of beauty both inside and out
　　has given the world her best
Now lives in the hearts of her family and friends,
　　I'm proud, Mom, you passed Life's test.

Haiku

Two friends
two cups
one pot of coffee

Child and dolly
high heels, hats and dresses
rainy afternoon

Toilet paper hangs
gray kittens alone all day
need no ball of yarn

Differentia

He cries heartrending tears,
but only in protected solitude—
concealing his real self.

Man's limitless power of endurance
by society's dictates
supports the masculine pride.

Dare he exhibit an emotion
of aching from within—
demonstrate honest feelings?
Ask not the macho man.

Painful

Oh scale of mine
why must you be
so sure and right
of the weight of me.

Your dial rests
upon that line
so quick to record
my every gain,

That when I stand
upon your back,
instead of you,
it gives me pain.

Carbon Copy

He's just a little duplicate—
A copy of his Dad;
His walk, his talk, his actions,
Like his father when a lad.

They are so very much alike,
They look one in the same;
They're identical in every way,
Why, even in their name!

You'd almost think that they were twins,
Except one is just a lad;
He's just a little duplicate—
A copy of his Dad.

Enlistment's Up

In selfish ecstasy
    I await the sacred setdown
    of the graceful, silver bird
    carrying one who served.

His chosen separation
    from commitments fulfilled.
Time demands
    yet another costume.

His returning—
    a process of renewal:
    cleansed of childhood.

My son returns a man.

Outdoor Concerts

I love the sounds of nature
And to hear her symphony,
Even without rehearsals
She plays in harmony.

Her bubbling brooks and chirping birds
Can make you want to sing,
The rustling leaves and whistling winds
In syncopation ring.

Her bullfrogs croak and cattails creak
On evenings by the ponds,
While playing tunes of outdoors
We know as nature's songs.

Her oceans roar while washing waves
Ashore on glistening sand
And scatters shells with sounds inside
Way up upon the land.

Her serenade of trickling rain
On rooftops in the night
Then gently puts her world to sleep
With essence of delight.

Haiku

Unraveling waves
gently scattering sea gifts
to summer shellers

Mouse in the kitchen
sounds of crinkling cellophane
cookies disappear

Blackberries on bush
picking season in summer
black bear and Gramma

Visions of Grandeur

I had high hopes that I would be
A dancer and my name you'd see
Flashed on marquees across the land
And dancing to some big name band.

To be real graceful on the floor
And dance with partners more and more.
I thought this fete would be a breeze
And I could learn to dance with ease.

But then it struck me quite a blow
When I discovered what I now know:
My legs are stiff and feet are flat
Instead like this, they go like that.

When someone asks me for a dance
It's only once—no second chance.
Next time I'll be polite to them
And say I will sit out this one.

Dorothy Blanchard Bennett

Dorothy Blanchard Bennett's writing and poetry is part of her therapeutic healing process. She shares her personal experiences in the hope that others can find their way as she has.

She has had much turmoil in her life and through therapy finds sharing comes easiest through writing her innermost feelings. She strongly believes people need to have more open and honest communication in all relationships and she is striving to improve her own personal relationships in this way.

Dorothy is single, has two grown children, two grandchildren and owns her own business. She is an avid lover of animals; has horses and tries to find time to go riding once a week.

She lives in Charlotte County, Florida.

My Child Within

It is hard for me, you see,
to verbally say what is within
so I have chosen to share
the only way I know how
with the words written down,
my feelings to show
which are coming from the deep
hidden parts of my mind.

Travel through my words
if you so choose
and you will probably find
where I have been
where I am now
and where I someday hope to be.

If you want to understand
it is here
and perhaps through me
you may also find
the child that is hidden within.

My Therapist

There are those close to me who believe
That a therapist is not what I need.
But they are definitely wrong in what they perceive.
I have been lucky beyond words
Because I have found my therapist to be
The best that has happened to me.
I truly believe that my therapist is blessed
That he is breathed on by a force from high above.
He always gives me all of his best
Compassion and understanding he does best
And he can sure put me to the test.
I just cannot imagine what might have happened to me
If he had not come into my life in my time of need.
Oh, he is just human for sure
And that is part of the cure.
He believed in me in ways I could not
He saw me as I thought no one should.
Oh, the patience it has taken
But we're not done yet!
It is so nice to know that I no longer walk alone.
So in closing, I would like to say
Thank you for coming my way
And thank you for calling me "friend."

Friends Should be Forever

My friend, what went wrong?
It took so many years to build what we had,
Only to be gone in such a short time.
The memories are so vivid, will they ever dim?
The hours spent in sharing...
dreaming dreams...listening...caring
and OH, the fantasies...
My friend, what went wrong?
I still miss you so...
I doubt that I will ever trust again just so,
You knew me so well - more so than anyone
Vulnerability now scares me so...
I don't blame you for my fears
They protect me from the tears.
I avoid places you would go—
Why I don't know.
Old friend I still miss you so...
There is comfort in hoping
That there are times in yourself
That you also feel as such.
Because if this is the case,
Then it all was not a waste.
Maybe someday again, my friend...

Childhoods

Did you have a childhood
At least one that you can recall?
Childhoods are suspended in time
   No matter how happy
   No matter how sad
A time that was so important
It is a shame that it is not understood.
But the mind has a way to block out
a day...a week...a year...
   or maybe it all...
Because sometimes it is the only way
To survive it all
As survival is the name of the game
From the day we are born
Until the very end...
So, if your childhood is gone
Or maybe missing within your mind
It might be that the mind needed
To lose it for a time
In order to survive it all...
I'm told that we can bring it all back
Maybe only a little at a time
It is all up to you...
I am told this will be painful to do
So it is entirely up to you...
Will your self-taught survival
   come into play
Or can you let go and work it through
To the very last day?

It is all up to you...
I'm told the rewards
Are worth fighting the battle for
but since it is all new to me
As I lost it all
I'm not sure I can start at all...

Peace

Peace is the magic
We all search for
The pot of gold
At the end of the rainbow.
Oh, yes elusive it is—
As elusive as anything you know.
There are times it comes and it goes
Just like a magic wand
Shaping your rainbow.
But we keep searching for the sweet glow,
As the taste is as sweet as honey you know.
To achieve a peace of mind in this life
Has got to be like finding
A pot of gold at the end of the rainbow!
I wish there were directions
That I could bestow,
But I, too, am chasing the pot of gold
At the end of my rainbow!

Incest Victims All

I sometimes wonder what it might have been like,
Had I not been an incest victim in the start of my life.
I know that I am not alone,
As there are many that have known
The horrors brought forth
By the lust of a sick mind
Relative of their own kind.
My childhood was lost by an action not mine
Only I am the one who has suffered
the pain, the guilt and the shame
Misplaced in my mind;
'Cause as I was only a child,
I could only be expected to think as such
And in my child's mind I was now dirty to touch.
The fears I held from day to day,
Were as real then as they are today.
What would happen if someone knew?
Would I be punished too?
Why does he threaten me so?
It leaves me with no place to go.
Who can I tell?
What will they do?
None yet has protected me from being misused.
Oh, Lord, what would happen if they knew?

He sneaks to my bed as I am sleeping away,
And what he does then
Would blow an adult away.
So how can you expect me to put it away

To never mention it again?
Forget what happened to me as a child?
You weren't that child who was blown away.
Sometime in my youth I blocked it all away
Somewhere deep in the depths of my mind;
Too ugly to look at
Much less to think about.
I tried to get into my adult life as such,
But I have found that somehow in the intricacies of my mind,
What happened to me way back in time
When I was just a child
Did not let me be all that should have been mine...
To bury things so deep
Still afraid and alone.
Can you possibly understand what it was like
When the memories seep up from below in an unending flow?
Who will ever understand—where do you go?
I only know I can't bury it any more.
It hurts so badly to see the pictures so clear.
I have no choice but to see,
The damage was done long before me.
I have to rid myself of the past
Which means to face it all in the
Flashes my mind chooses not to suppress...
In time, hopefully it will end,
And then I will be able to accept
What happened to me as a child is gone at last.
Then maybe, I hope, I will find
The person inside who is truly my friend...

I Don't Clean Windows

(For C.M.)

I don't clean windows,
why is this so?
I don't want to see
through to the dirt anymore.
It's easier you see,
to stay inside,
Not able to look
through to the outside.
I have been told
that once you wash just one window clean,
That then it will be
hard not to continue to clean.
The question I have, though,
am I afraid to look out,
Or am I just afraid for others to see in?
Or maybe, just maybe so,
I am afraid
that I will have to then look into my soul.
It seems to me,
that all is inside, and that is why,
I sometimes find,
that it is so difficult to step outside.
The fact is, though,
that those windows do need to be cleaned,
not only from within, but also outside the door.
I guarantee you this,
the desire is strong,
from deep within my soul
To really get it done;
So then I could say,
I don't <u>need</u> to clean windows no more!

Pain

Pain is something
That I do not like to talk about
As it is always following me about
Where it came from I just do not know
And why it stays with me
Seems beyond my control...
The feeling is hard to explain
To rid myself of the pain.
I know I am not alone in this dilemma
That is beyond my control
But to reach out is so hard to do,
But reach out I must
In order to rid myself of its hold.
If you would just help me
Along this bumpy road,
Maybe together we can control the pain
That has put us on hold.
Hang on!
We can make it I'm sure
Together through the tangled maze of pain.
There has to be
An end to it all someday.
The answers are deep within
Just come with me to the end...

"Mother"

You came into my life so many years ago
When we were both so much younger for sure
It amazes me now as it did then
That your acceptance of me was so
Immediate and genuine.
Oh I knew from the start
That there was no real love that had begun
But throughout these years that have
Passed between us
The love also came and grew
As each passing season.
We have shared so much, you and I
In fact the memories would reach to the sky
You have given me so much
Words just cannot express
What you have meant to me as time has gone by
Your son brought me to you
    but since then he has left
You have given me the best memories yet...
I remember how pleased you were
When I brought with me
The only little girl there was to be --
Your princess.

You loved her immediately and that shows
What a special person you are.
Do you remember holding my hand
When I gave birth to your very first grandson?
The look on your face as you held him first
Was a joy to me beyond words
Oh yes, Mother, there have been many
        bridges that we have crossed together
As the years have come and gone...
The children are all grown
And we are left with more memories by far
Too numerous to begin to express
But they are there, within our hearts.
I many times have wished
        that I could have been blessed
To have been a child in your arms...
But I am thankful to have known you at all
And more grateful than you'll ever know
To be called your "daughter"
Instead of your "daughter-in-law!"
Mother, I LOVE YOU SO!

We Are There For You

There really are no words
to help you get through
this difficult time
that you are going through...

I wish there was a way
I could make the pain go away
but, my friend, the secret to that
lies in you...

The answers are such
that no one can give them to you.
Give yourself time,
It will come to you.
But if it will help,
Just remember that...you are not alone
In this struggle you are going through.

There is not anyone
who can fix all that is wrong,
But what we can do
is to be there for you...

You will have to reach out
as we know not what you need
It is all up to you
To let us be there...
We are more than willing
to walk with you
Through this difficult time for you...

There are some things in this life
that seem just too painful to bear
and it helps to have
a friend to share...

We all are aware
That the good times are so easy to enjoy
With those with whom we are close...
But we find it more difficult
to express the pain that is inside...

But, my friend, I have learned
That the only hope is to find
A shoulder that you can lean on
To help you through these difficult times
So please, just remember this
We are there for you...

My Children

I have two children
Now grown with lives of their own.
Words cannot express
How special they each are to me.
I am proud beyond words
Of the person they each have become...

We have a special relationship
We three...
Some who see
Do not understand where it comes from.

In these years now past
We have truly been through a lot
We three...
It created a bond
As strong as can be
Built on a genuine love and trust
Between us three...

We each know
That there are always two more
That will be there
When the need is such.

I look and listen
To others complain and moan
About the troubles they endure
With the children that are their own.
It makes me humble
In the pride I feel
When I think of my two children
And the knowledge of the adult
That they each have become...

I could leave this world tomorrow
And know
I succeeded with two goals
In this, my life on earth.

A Tragedy—or— Miracle?

Another tragedy hit
As lightning came down
And struck three of our horses
To the ground.
We fought to help them survive
        as best we could, but the miracle was
        that they again stood.
In the throes of it all,
While trying to keep
Each horse as calm as could be,
   and waiting for the vet to arrive,
I looked at the sky
And was amazed to see
A sunset too beautiful to describe.
I found myself becoming mesmerized and calmed
By the beauty it held
In the midst of this tragedy.
Throughout the night
        these horses fought to survive
        with a will not to die.
Morning did come
And they all three were still alive;
        damaged, yes,
The final outcome still unknown.

All that can now be done
Is to simply take each day
   one by one.
Through this all I really believe
There is a lesson for each of us
That was there to surmise.
I really have to wonder
Was this really a tragedy,
Or were we observing a miracle
As it was happening...
We all could gain
As we watched in vain,
The simple process of
The deep animal need
In just wanting to survive,
In spite of the pain...
I hope others can understand
What this could all mean
If put in a perspective of their lives.
But, if not, I must surmise,
That maybe they would have had to be there
To actually witness the scene
   unfold before their eyes
To be able to question again
What it could all mean.

Rainbows

Recently I observed
An absolutely perfect rainbow.
The arch of colors reached across the sky,
So brilliant that it could not help
But catch and hold your eye.
It is rare indeed to see
A rainbow so perfect and complete
With no discrepancies in it to see.
The colors varied and bright
In fact, more colors than you would ordinarily see
In a rainbow in the sky.
The other amazing thing I realized
As I stood mesmerized by this beautiful perfect
Sight before my eyes,
Was the length of time this rainbow stayed visible
        in the sky.
I have found that most rainbows that do appear
Are usually not there to enjoy for too long a time
Or I find they seem to change colors or shapes
        before your eyes.
They are not usually a perfect arch across the sky,

Nor is their brilliance
Always enough to catch and hold a person's eye,
But this one rainbow was
The rare, perfect, brilliant rainbow
That was there for each that cared
To stop and behold the beauty of it all.
I had to surmise as I was standing there
These thoughts held a message within
Life is really not so different than
Each rainbow that appears in the sky, as

> There are changes
> There are times not so perfect
> Times it is not all clear
> Times that feel like unbroken patterns
> Times that life feels brilliant from within
> Our lives an unbroken pattern
> > From beginning to end,
> And of course, the eternal hope to find
> That magical pot of gold at the end of the
> > Rainbow.

But there are always times
That it does all come together
To just feel perfect and right
And times, too,
That this good feeling will last
Longer than usual.

All in the Mind?

I find it so hard to comprehend
Why there is such a difference
In the way some look at an illness
That is situated in the mind
From an illness that has
Ravaged a body from within.

Has our society still not yet
Come far enough along
For us to accept
That an illness in the mind,
Emotional problems uncontrolled,
Can do as much damage
In an individual life
As a cancer that eats away
At a body that once was whole

Maybe someday this will change
And people will understand
The damage that can be wrought,
By all in contact with
An illness out of control
But situated in the mind
Not in the body as a whole.

Other titles available from Tabby House Books.

 TABBY HOUSE BOOKS

4429 Shady Lane, Charlotte Harbor, FL 33980
813-629-7646 • 813-627-6938

Send me:

☐ **Read My Lips: No New Pets** $8.⁹⁵
Award-winning humor by
Linda Grotke Salisbury

☐ **Good-bye Tomato, Hello Florida** $8.⁹⁵
Outstanding humor by
Linda Grotke

☐ **The Creatures Nobody Loves** $3.⁹⁵
Everett W. Newcomb, Jr.
Corky Crocodile and friends learn their
importance in God's world. Subtle
lessons in mutual respect, courtesy,
self-esteem and acceptance. Centerfold
of animals to color. Juvenile 8-10 ys.

☐ **While Morning Stars Sang** $7.⁹⁵
Six contemporary poets share love of
language, humor, spirituality, philosophy,
healing, pain and life experiences.

☐ **Bought With A Price** $6.⁹⁵
Peggy Albrecht
Romance and adventure for a young American
woman in Africa. Written by a former missionary
and author of four books for young people,
Albrecht vividly brings to life the calling to the
mission field, challenges of adapting to a new land
and romantic longings of her heroine.

Send a check or money order with this coupon:
(I'm adding $2⁰⁰ per book for postage and handling
and 6% sales tax for Florida residents.)

Send my books to (please print)

Name _____

Address _____

City _____ State _____ Zip _____